# Witold Lutosławski

# CONCERTO
# FOR ORCHESTRA

## CHESTER MUSIC

(A division of Music Sales Limited)

This work was first performed on November 26th, 1954 by the Warsaw Philharmonic Orchestra conducted by Witold Rowicki.

|     |                                    | Page |
|-----|------------------------------------|------|
| I   | Intrada                            | 1    |
| II  | Capriccio, Notturno e Arioso       | 31   |
| III | Passacaglia, Toccata e Corale      | 61   |

## ORCHESTRATION

3   Flutes (II & III doubling Piccolos)
3   Oboes (III doubling Cor Anglais)
3   Clarinets in A and B♭ (III doubling Bass Clarinet in B♭)
3   Bassoons (III doubling Double Bassoon)
4   Horns in F
4   Trumpets in C
4   Trombones
1   Tuba
2   Harps
1   Piano
1   Celeste
4   Timpani
Percussion (3 players):
     Side Drum with snares
     3 Side Drums without snares (high, medium and low)
     Tenor Drum
     Bass Drum
     3 Cymbals
     Tam-Tam
     Tambourine
     Xylophone
     Glockenspiel
Strings

Orchestral material on hire
Duration c.29 minutes

*Witoldowi Rowickiemu*

# CONCERTO FOR ORCHESTRA

Witold Lutoslawski
1954

## I

## INTRADA

CH55276

4
Fl. I II III
f agressivo
Ob. I II III
Cl. in la I III
Fg. I II
Cor. in fa I II III IV
poco sf pp
sf pp
Tmp.
poco sf
Ar. I, II
Vni I
f
sf
mf
4 soli Vni II altri
pp
4 sole Vle altre
pp
4 soli Vc. altri
f
pp
Cb.
4

11

_a tempo, ma quieto_

# II
## CAPRICCIO NOTTURNO
### E
## ARIOSO

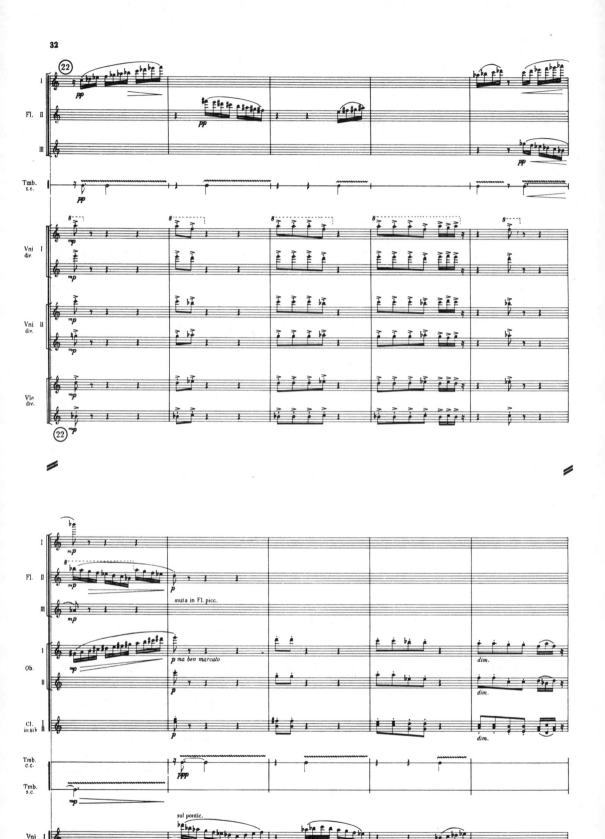

P.G. ㉞

P.G.

㉞

9 Stesso movimento (𝅗𝅥. = ♩♩♩ = 57)
Fl.p.
Fl. I II
Ob. I II III
Cl. in la I II
a2
Cl.b. in si♭
muta in Cl.III in la
Fg. I II
Cfg.
Cor. in fa I II III IV
Tr. in do I II III IV
ff cantando
quasi legato
senza sord.
Trbn. I II III IV
(a2)
Tb.
Tmb. c.c.
Tmb. s.c.
Tmb. rull.
Pfte
senza Ped.
9 Stesso movimento
div.
unis.
Vni I II
Vle div.
Vc. div.
Cb.

52

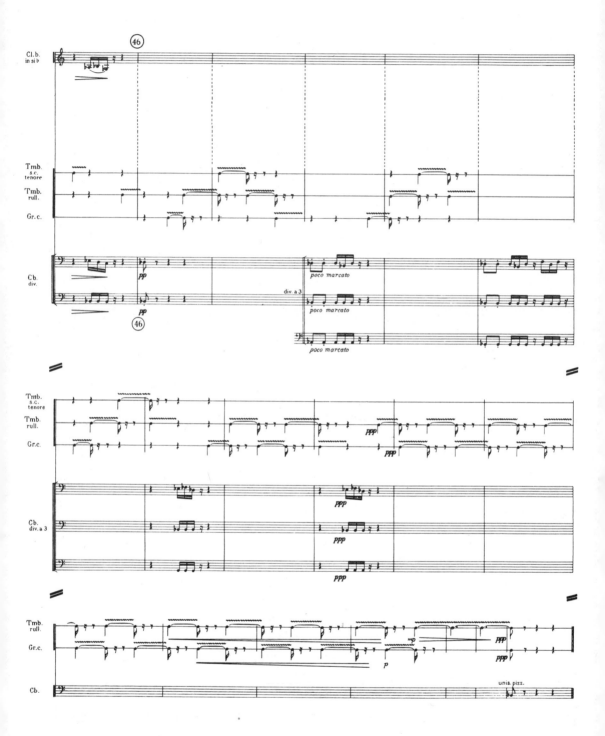

# III

## PASSACAGLIA
## TOCCATA E CORALE

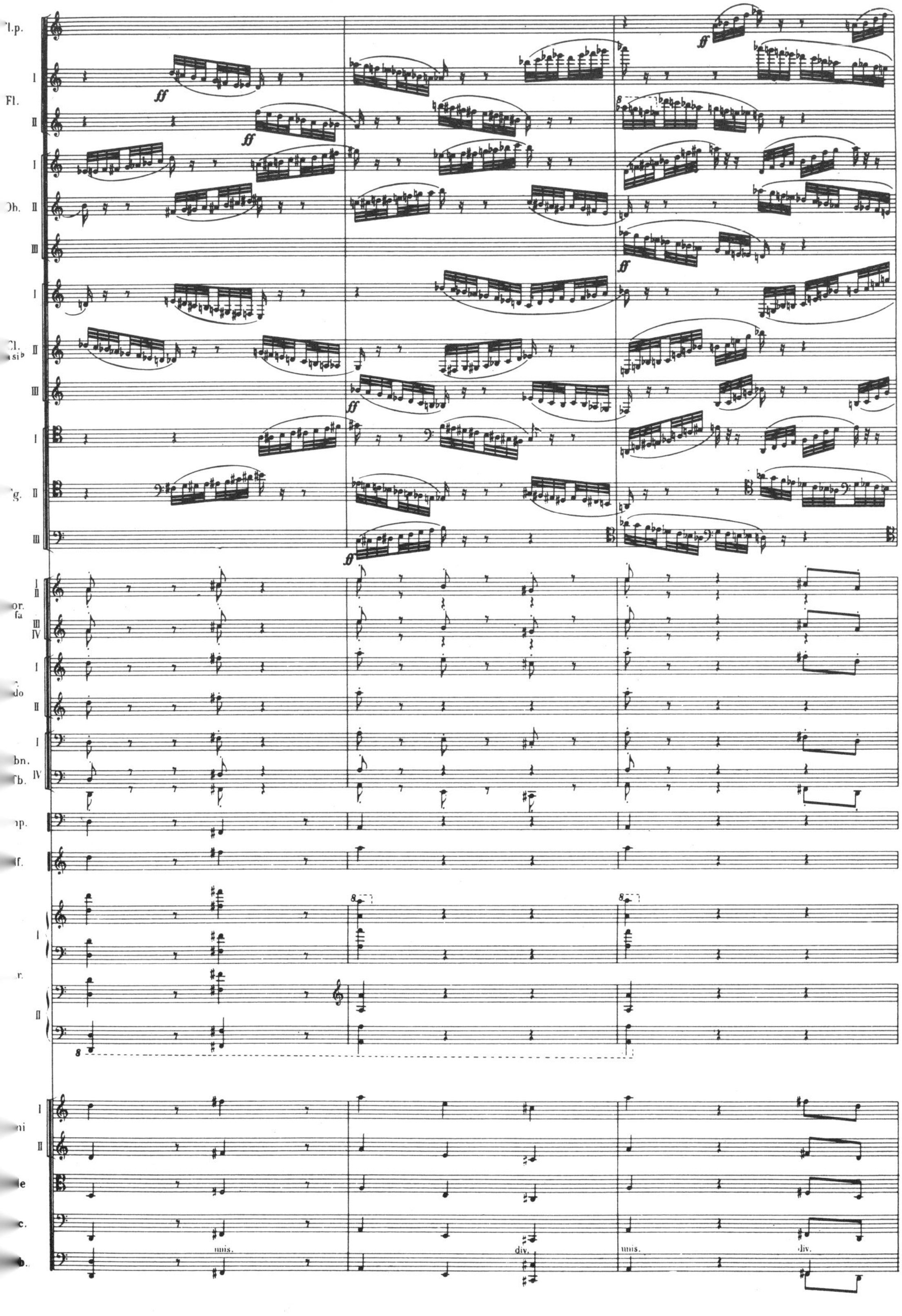
Fl.p.
Fl.
Ob.
Cl. sib
Fg.
Cor. fa
do
Tbn. Tb.
Af.
ff
unis.
div.

Fl.p.
Fl. I II
a2
Cl. in si♭ I
II III
Fg. I II
Cfg.
Cor. in fa I II
III
IV
Tr. in do I
II
III
IV
Trbn. IV e Tb.
Tmp.
Pfte
Vni I
unis.
Vni II
Vle div.
Vc.
div.
Cb.
ff
f
cresc.
fp
mf

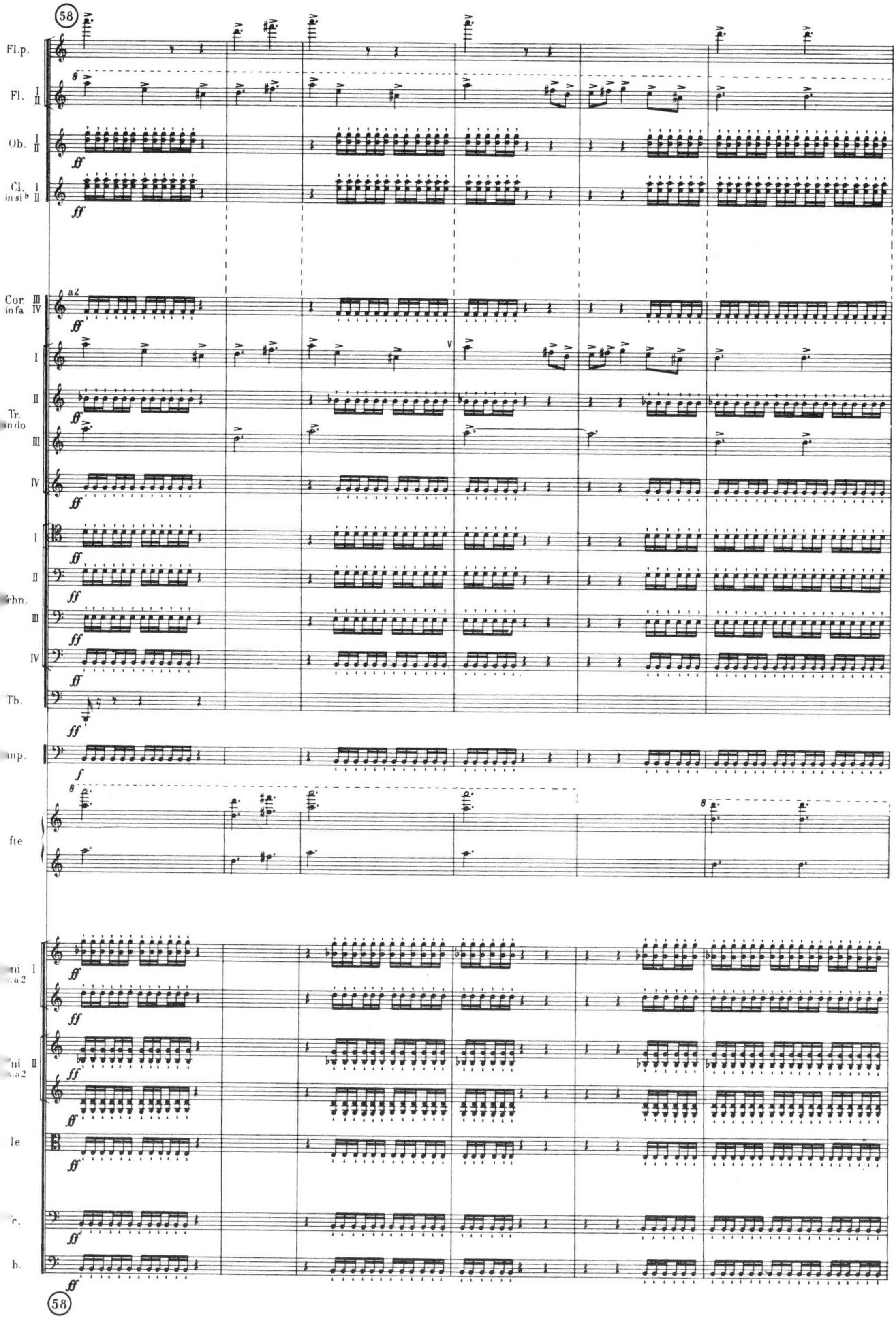
58
Fl.p.
Fl. I II
Ob. I II
Cl. I II in si♭
Cor. III IV in fa
a2
Tr. in do
I
II
III
IV
Tb.
fte
ff
f
58

Fg. I II
Cor. in fa I II III IV
Tr. in do I II
Vni I II
Vle
Vc.
Cb.
simile
simile
64
Cl. in si♭ I II III
a 3
Cfg.
a 2
Trbn. I II III IV
Tb.
Pfte
con Ped.
div.
unis.

94

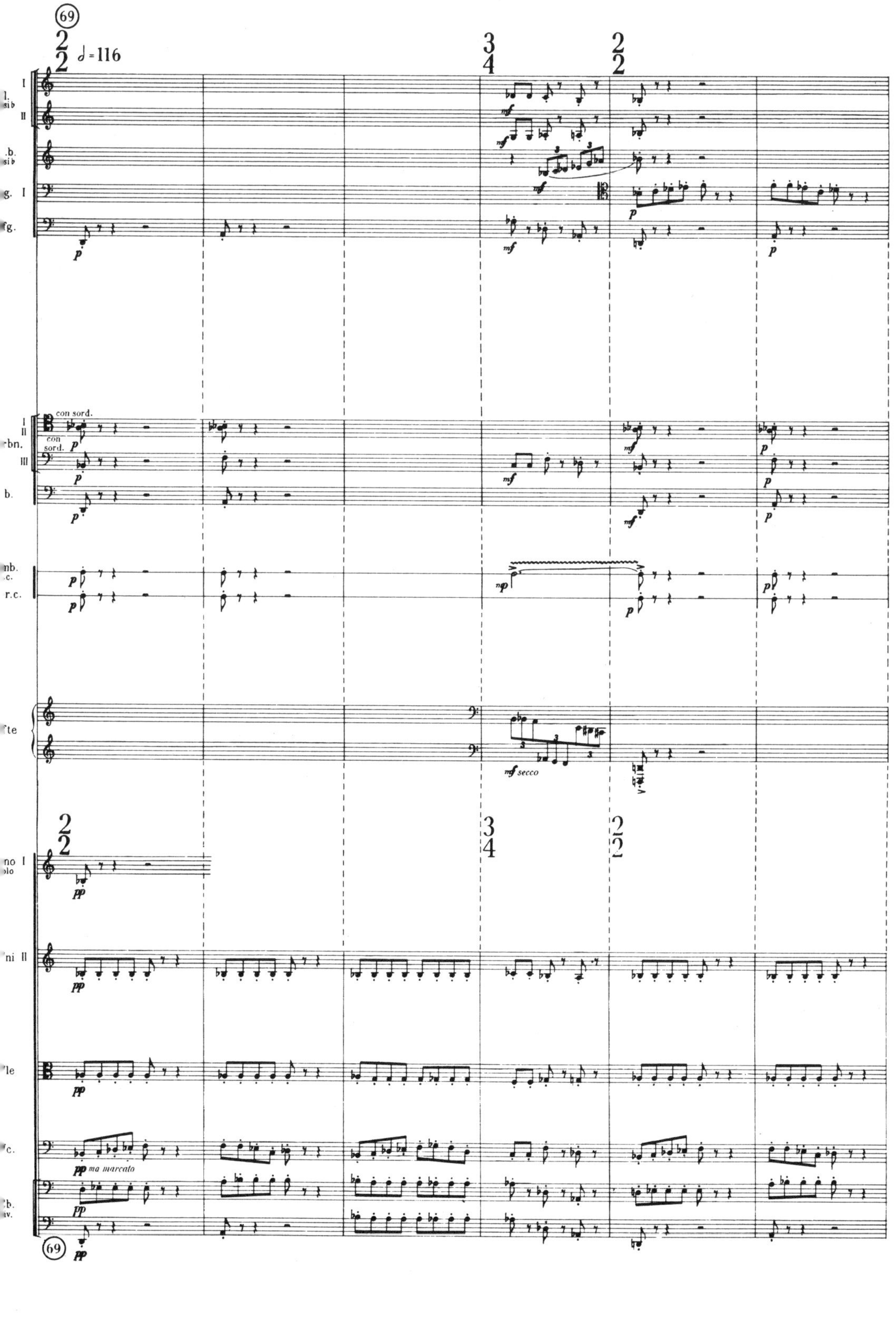
69
𝅗𝅥 = 116
con sord.
con sord.
mf secco
pp ma marcato
69

126

Fl.p.
Fl.
Ob.
Cl. in si♭
Fg.
Cfg.
Cor. in fa
Trbn.
Tb.
Tmp.
Ptto
Tmb. s.c.
Pfte
Vni
Vle
Vc.
Cb.
(a2)
ff
p
poco f
(div.)

poco avvivando
Fl.p. I II
Fl. I
Ob. I II III
Cl. in si♭ I II III
Fg. I II
Cfg.
Cor in fa I II III IV
Tr. in do I II III IV
Trbn. I II III
Tb.
Tmb. rull.
Ar. I II
mi♮, fa♮
poco avvivando
Vni I
1 solo Vni II altri
1 sola Vle altre
(pizz.)
div.
Vc.
pizz.
Cb.

# Quasi stesso movimento ( ♩=♩.=136)

Quasi stesso movimento

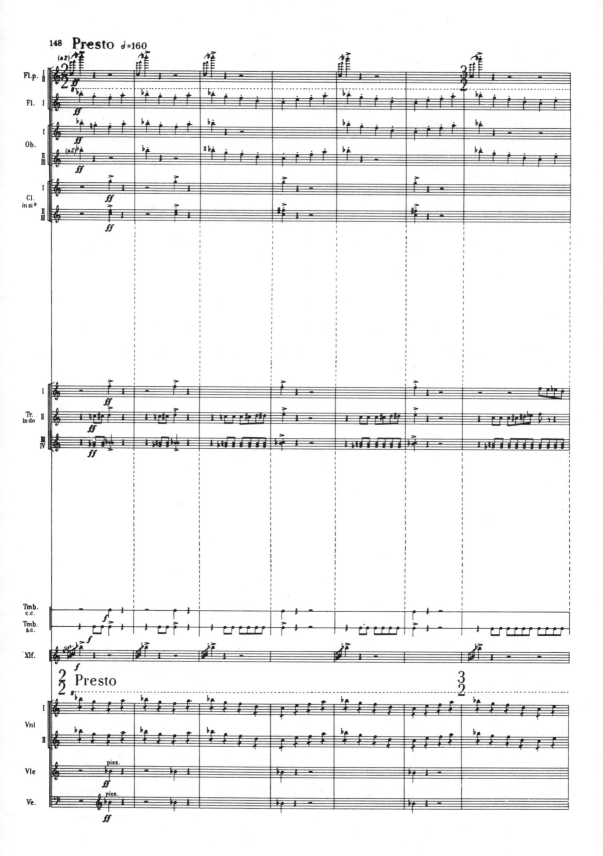

150

Printed and bound in Great Britain by
Caligraving Limited Thetford Norfolk

12/03 (49650)